BUGATTI

KING OF THE CLASSICS

BY JAY SCHLEIFER

Crestwood House
New York
Maxwell Macmillan Canada
Toronto
Maxwell Macmillan International
New York   Oxford   Singapore   Sydney

Crestwood House
Macmillan Publishing Company
866 Third Avenue
New York, NY 10022

Maxwell Macmillan Canada, Inc.
1200 Eglinton Avenue East
Suite 200
Don Mills, Ontario M3C 3N1

Macmillan Publishing Company is part of the Maxwell Communication
Group of Companies.

First Edition
Produced by Twelfth House Productions
Designed by R Studio T

Printed in the United States of America

10 9 8 7 6 5 4 3 2 1

Library of Congress Cataloging-in-Publication Data

Schleifer, Jay.
    Bugatti / by Jay Schleifer.—1st ed.
        p.   cm.—(Cool classics)
    Summary: Traces the history and popularity of the Bugatti, which
    has been dubbed the European king of customized cars.
                ISBN 0-89686-813-3
    1. Bugatti automobile—History—Juvenile literature.   [1. Bugatti
    automobile—History.]   I. Title.   II. Series.
            TL215.B82S35   1994
                629.2'092—dc20   93-15491
                        [B]

CONTENTS

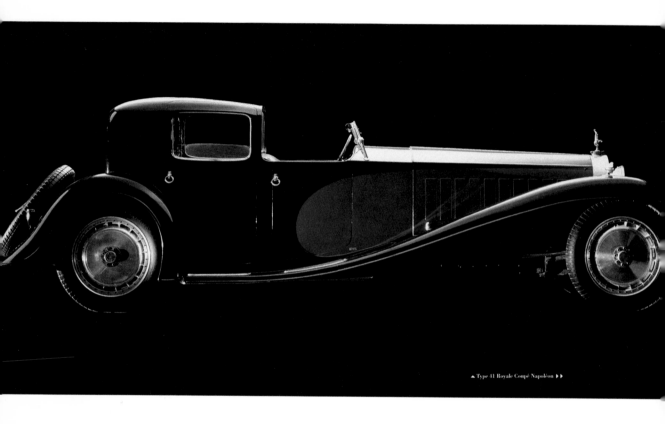

▲ Type 41 Royale Coupé Napoléon ▶▶

Meet the king of cars, the Type 41 Bugatti Royale!

4

1 THE MOST VALUABLE CAR IN THE WORLD

It's the night of nights for car collectors. Hundreds gather in the ballroom of a fancy hotel. Dressed in the finest clothes, they arrive in limousines. Wealth and power are their trademarks. They've come to attend the yearly classic car auction. And each guest hopes to leave with one of the finest cars ever built.

You've probably seen an auction. First an item is brought out to be viewed. Then the auctioneer asks the buyers how much they'll pay for it. The buyers bid by shouting out an amount or raising a hand when the auctioneer calls out a price. In the end, the buyer willing to pay the most is the one who gets the item.

Car auctions are held all the time. But this night is different. Tonight, expensive cars like Ferraris and Rolls-Royces are on the auction block. The buyers are the top car collectors in the world. A Ferrari is no big deal to them. They often buy or sell such cars.

But now, as the auction nears its end, the room begins to buzz with excitement. The car that's about to go on sale is a big deal to them—a very big deal! Until now, that car has been behind a curtain, watched by armed guards. Now it's ready to roll into view.

"Ladies and gentlemen," says the auctioneer. "The moment I know you've all been waiting for is here. Coming in from your right—the Type 41 Bugatti Royale!" As jaws drop, one of the most incredible wheeled machines ever built is pushed onto the stage. The car is so long that its hood alone seems to stretch from New York to Paris. And you could park another car in the 14 feet between its front and rear wheels!

It's heavy, weighing in at more than 3 tons. It takes a full crew to push the car onto the platform.

It's sleek, despite its age of close to 60 years.

And it's unusual, especially the engine. Under the endless hood lives one of the largest engines ever to power an automobile—a straight eight of 12.7 **liters.** It's the size of three modern V-8s!

Most important to the people in this room, the car is rare. Only six Royales were ever built. Each one is a masterpiece.

To collectors everywhere, Bugatti is a magic name. And this is the most magical of Bugattis. The bidding begins in the low millions of dollars.

It doesn't stay there long. As the auctioneer eggs buyers on, hands wave, and the millions multiply. At 4 million, some of those hands go limp. At 5 million, almost all have sunk back into the crowd, but a few wave on. These are the major players—bidders rich enough to have flown here in their own jets. They want this car.

Finally, the auctioneer shouts the cry of "going, going, GONE!" and both the car and a fortune change hands. The Royale has been sold for an incredible $9.8 MILLION! It's the highest price ever paid for an automobile. For this sum of money, you could buy a complete high school—gym, band room, and all.

Amazingly, nobody in the crowd knows who the buyer is. He or she has chosen to make the deal through an agent. Maybe it's a pro ball player, a rock star, the owner of a giant company, or even a king or queen. The mystery adds to the excitement.

As soon as the money reaches the bank, the car disappears into a special bulletproof, fireproof truck, guarded by police. Then the little caravan takes off. The Bugatti may not be sold again for years. But the next time it does go on sale, one thing is sure: It will sell for even more money.

What is it about this monstrously big 60-year-old hunk of metal and glass, leather and rubber, that makes it worth the price of a large building, or even a small town? What's the magic behind the name Bugatti?

Read on and find out.

2 "LE PATRON"

The fantastic Bugatti Royale was built by a man who was almost royal himself. His name was Ettore Bugatti (Ay-TOR-ray Boo-GAH-tee). He lived and worked in France during the first half of the twentieth century. And he was as much a king as he was an automaker.

As an automaker, Bugatti had a car factory. But just as a king builds his empire around him, Ettore built his factory on his large estate. The property was also home to his collections of art, racehorses, and hunting dogs.

Like any automaker, Bugatti employed a staff. But his workers were treated more like loyal family members. They were told to follow any command he gave them, without question. They even had a special name for their boss. They called him **Le Patron.** In French it means something like "Master," or "the Boss."

Can you imagine American automakers calling their bosses "Master"? Not likely! But not only did Bugatti's workers use this title for their boss—most felt that it was a special honor to work for him.

Finally, like any automaker, Bugatti followed the basic rules of auto design. But like a king, he also felt free to build cars that pleased him. He didn't have to please his buyers. If people wanted one of his cars, fine. If not, that was *their* problem, not his. Bugatti was able to get away with doing what he wanted because he was a true design genius, with ideas far ahead of their times.

Ettore Bugatti was born on September 15, 1881, near Milan, in northern Italy. During his growing-up years, he was heavily influenced by his father, Carlo Bugatti.

Carlo was an artist. He painted, sculpted, and created beautiful furniture for a living. Carlo saw himself as part of a line of artists going back to the great masters of the 1500s. Perhaps to

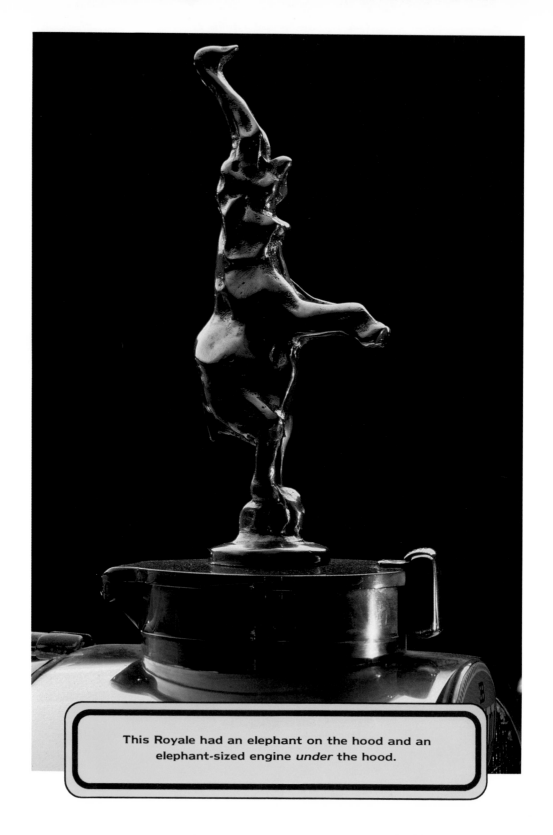

This Royale had an elephant on the hood and an elephant-sized engine *under* the hood.

8

honor such artists, he named Ettore's younger brother Rembrandt.

Ettore was proud of his father. "When an object left his hand," he wrote later, "he made it all that it was…from the rough block of material to the finished work." Ettore used that same idea when he built cars. He would mold his own creations. He, and only he, would take the raw materials and turn them into amazing machines.

In such a family it was natural that the children would take up art. Both young Ettore and his brother, Rembrandt, played with paintbrushes and carving tools. But Carlo's talent hadn't flowed equally to his sons. Rembrandt was blessed with artistic talent. He became a master sculptor. Ettore, on the other hand, found that no matter how hard he tried, he couldn't match the talent of either his brother or his father. Art would not be his path to fame.

Fortunately for Ettore, Milan was a major Italian factory city. In the 1880s and 1890s, the streets were alive with new inventions. One smoking, belching wheeled contraption was a machine called a *maquina,* or motorcar.

In those early days of the automobile, nobody was quite sure what such a device should be like. No one knew whether it should have steam or gasoline power, have one engine or more, or even if it should have three wheels or four.

Young Ettore was fascinated with the machine. Somehow he pulled together enough money to buy a motor tricycle. Although he had no idea how to operate or drive the three-wheeled machine, Ettore tried it out. His experience led to a job with a local machine shop that built such devices. And after he'd done some learning, Ettore built his own car—a three-wheeler with two engines. He was only 17 years old.

In 1898, this was an incredible achievement for a young man with little training. At the time, even top engineers were mystified by motor vehicles.

Here's Ettore Bugatti's first vehicle. A separate engine powers each rear wheel.

Ettore entered his little home-built car in ten local races. He won eight of them. Then he went on to enter his car in a major race held in France. He placed well in that competition, too. And he was racing against some of the top drivers of the day!

It was clear that Ettore had found his art. But unlike his father or brother, *his* masterpieces would be made of steel *and* powered by gasoline.

On returning to Milan, Bugatti built other odd cars. One strange vehicle had four engines—one for each wheel! But Ettore had to find a new workshop. The company he'd been with had decided its future lay in making sewing machines.

That led Ettore to an important decision. While the vehicles he built were strange and fun, they were not very useful. If he was to make it in the auto business, he had to design a car that people wanted to buy.

Young Ettore returned to his drawing board. And when he finally put his pencil down, he'd made auto history. The little car he designed, without help from anyone, had an **overhead valve engine**—a design other automakers didn't catch up with for years. It also had a four-speed gearbox and a new electrical system. While endless hand cranking was needed for other cars, Ettore's machine started easily because of this electric system. It could also cruise all day at the then breakneck speed of 40 miles per hour. The car was a marvel.

Even more of a marvel was the way Bugatti had designed it. "The idea grew in my mind," he said later, "and went from there to my drawing board and then to metal. It was perfect at birth. Once done, it needed no changes."

Shown at the 1901 Milan Auto Show, this first real Bugatti car caused a stir among managers from the top auto companies. One executive, De Dietrich of Germany, offered Ettore a major job. As chief engineer, Ettore would oversee the design of all the company's cars for the next seven years. The company said he would be paid a hefty sum for each car sold from his designs, and even more if the cars were racers.

The job offer was fabulous. There was really only one problem. Bugatti had to get his father to sign the contract. At age 19, De Dietrich's new chief engineer was too young legally to sign it!

The car that got Bugatti his first big job had chain drive. "Le Patron," seen here at the wheel, wasn't even 19 when he created it.

3 THE MASTER OF MOLSHEIM

Bugatti left his native Italy to join De Dietrich in Germany. He lived in several cities before he settled in an area called Alsace.

Alsace is on the border between Germany and France and has belonged to both countries. Over history, whenever the two nations had a war, the victor ended up with Alsace.

When Bugatti moved there, Alsace was German. A few years later, after World War I, it became part of France again. Which of the three nations would get Bugatti's loyalty? Bugatti was born Italian, but he had lived in Germany, then later in France.

France got his vote. For the rest of his life, Bugatti spoke French. He followed French ways and painted his racers bright blue, the racing color of France.

The city he settled in was Molsheim (MOLTZ-hime). If you say "Molsheim" to a car lover, Bugatti's name leaps to mind.

Bugatti's contract with De Dietrich called for seven years of work. But Ettore never got used to the way big companies do business. The top executives frequently clashed with the willful young engineer, who wanted to do things his way.

So it was no surprise that, in 1909, Bugatti struck out on his own again. Using borrowed money, he started a new company in an old dye works. He had fewer than 100 employees—a tiny factory compared with giant De Dietrich. But this time, Ettore Bugatti told himself, the cars would be done his way...or no way.

4 LIGHTER IS BETTER

From the time the place opened, anyone visiting the Bugatti works at Molsheim instantly saw that it was a different kind of car factory.

For one thing, it was also Bugatti's home. He'd settled there with his wife, two daughters, and his young son, Jean. Another son, Roland, was born later.

The factory itself was a collection of workshops, each kept incredibly clean. There was none of the usual grit and grime found around places where machine work is done.

There were other differences as well. Job titles were not important at the Bugatti works. There was no chain of bosses and managers. Everyone seemed to have his or her job to do, but nobody took orders from anyone but Mr. Bugatti himself.

Everyone took *his* orders, though, to the letter! Workers who disobeyed were quickly fired or would leave on their own. The group soon became like a second family to Bugatti, with the master at its head. Le Patron was very much like a father to these loyal employees.

Yet it didn't seem to be the fear of getting fired that produced this loyalty. Instead, each worker seemed to understand that he or she had been given a chance to learn from a true genius.

One lesson the workers learned quickly was the importance of lightweight vehicles. Bugatti had a strong belief in keeping the vehicles he designed as light as possible. This idea was totally opposite to the opinion of most engineers of the day. They thought weight added to a car's ability to hold the road, and they piled on the pounds. The argument would be decided on the racetrack.

In mid-1911, an unusual new racer rolled from the Molsheim works. Compared with the giant, 2-ton machines of the day, it was tiny, weighing in at only about 700 pounds. There was hardly enough room for the crew of driver and mechanic. In fact, mechanics had to carry the spare tire in their arms because they had no other place to put it!

Trucked to the famous track at **Le Mans,** the new car was **15**

The "Baby Bugatti" racer won by stripping away
extra weight.

greeted with laughter at first. Drivers called it Baby Bugatti. They said that a machine that delicate could never stand up to the strain of racing. But race day turned out to be incredibly hot. Soon the lurching 2-ton cars were breaking down. Tires melted, axles snapped, and brakes broke. The smoking, belching monsters skidded around the turns, barely under control.

In comparison, Ettore's "Baby" tiptoed through the mess. The driver barely had to change gears as he brought the brand-new car to a solid second-place finish. The little car had averaged more than 56 miles per hour over 402 miles of racing.

This near win—against some of the world's great car companies—showed how advanced Bugatti's ideas were. As soon as the news hit the papers, orders started to pour into Molsheim for both road cars and racecars.

Some of these orders came from Europe's royal families. Overnight, Bugatti was becoming both rich and famous. He was making powerful friends, too.

Bugatti's wealthy customers gave him a financial advantage. Bugatti did not have to spend all his time making thousands of low-priced cars. Instead, he could charge a high price, sell a few cars to keep the bills paid, and devote the rest of the time to designing and building what he wanted. In all the years he ran the factory, from 1910 to 1947, Bugatti built about 8,000 cars. Only 700 of them were racers. Any one of the world's major car companies builds almost 8,000 cars in a single day!

Within a very short time, that second-place finish was replaced by the company's first wins. There was success in business, too, and the factory was growing. It seemed that nothing could get in his way.

But something soon would. The year was 1914. World War I was about to start. It would turn Bugatti's happy world totally upside down!

 WAR AND PEACE

With a war brewing between France and Germany, Molsheim was exactly the wrong place to be. The little city sat right in the path of the armies of both nations. It didn't matter which side won. Molsheim was going to get rolled over.

Bugatti knew this. And as soon as the armies began to march, so did he. "We're moving!" he told his work force, now close to 400 strong. As fast as they could, Bugatti's workers packed everything they could. There was no way to save the larger machines. They were too bulky to be taken from the factory without special cranes. But half-built cars could be driven to safety, as long as they had enough parts attached to run.

As it happened, five brand-new racers were in the works. Employees hurriedly completed two of them and sped out of the factory gates, just beating the guns and army tanks already on the way. The other three machines were stripped down. Their parts were wrapped in oil-soaked protective paper. Then they were buried. The three racers lay under the ground for four years, like seeds of speed waiting to bloom. When the war ended, they needed only to be dug up, cleaned off, and reassembled to get the Bugatti company back into the racecar business.

Bugatti and his family left by train, looking for a place to live safely. They finally ended up in Paris. There Ettore offered his services to the French government. He was put to work designing aircraft engines.

His successes included a **double eight,** in which two eight-cylinder engines used one set of larger parts. This arrangement gave the plane twice the power at about half the weight.

When the war ended, Bugatti returned to his beloved Molsheim. Amazingly, the factory was not heavily damaged. And the three buried cars were exactly where they'd been left. Bugatti was able to return immediately to racing. His team won the only major race run in France in 1920—at the famed Le Mans track. But that victory happened as much in spite of Bugatti as because of him.

As the cars rounded the track and came into the pits for gas, Bugatti suddenly had the feeling that a radiator cap on one racer had not been well tightened. He reached over the railing and checked it. His car was instantly thrown out of the race by the officials. Only mechanics were allowed to touch the cars, not owners.

The crowd hissed. Bugatti glowered. But one of his other cars won.

This victory was to be repeated many times during the years between World War I and World War II. In that era, no maker won as steadily as Bugatti. Other teams had a few good years. But when they faded, as they always did, Bugatti was still there, adding to an incredible total of wins and high-place finishes. From 1924 to 1927 alone, Bugatti cars collected close to 2,000 race wins!

One reason, of course, was that Ettore built great cars. But another was that he really didn't care who owned the winning machine. Whether the car was owned by his factory or by one of his customers, Bugatti was happy if it carried the famous red oval "EB" nameplate.

This was a very different way of thinking. Other teams kept the best cars for themselves. They sold the hand-me-downs to customers. Bugatti raced his best, but he also sold his best. So there were always lots of top Bugatti racers on the track. If the factory ran into bad luck, a customer might well save the day.

One of the most interesting designs was the famous 1923 **Tank** racer—a low, long creature that looked as much like a speedboat or a submarine as a car. Other racers still had much of the wagonlike look of early cars. But Bugatti's Tank marked one of the first uses of modern streamlining. Its wheels were inside the body shell. Its nose was low and sloped. And its tail was stretched and rounded for smooth airflow.

The car wasn't perfect, of course. It had high-speed handling problems. The reason was that Bugatti really didn't understand **19**

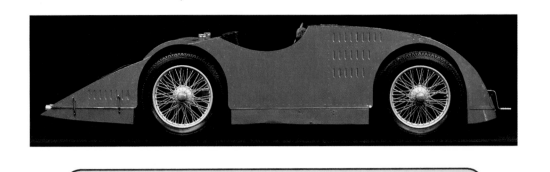

There are no extras on the Type 32 Tank. Just bare-bones mechanical parts.

streamlining. He'd designed the Tank body to work better in the wind, but it worked too well. The body was acting like an aircraft wing, lifting the car off the track.

In another brainstorm, Bugatti came up with the idea of running the exhaust pipe out the back of the body. This self-made wind could add to the car's speed. Had the plan worked, his car would have seemed to be partly jet-powered, and it looked every bit the part! With its unusual shape, this car is called the Cigar. But exhaust gas flows too slowly to add much power.

But just as Bugatti was willing to experiment, he also could be backward in his thinking. One example concerned **independent front suspension.** In this design, the front wheels are attached separately to the car so that if one wheel hits a bump, the other stays steady on the road. Even as other carmakers began to use this improvement, Bugatti refused to do so. Instead, he stuck with an old-fashioned **solid axle** design left over from horse-drawn-wagon days.

He also refused, for years, to use **hydraulic brakes.** In this system the brake pedal pumps a liquid to make the brakes work. Instead, Bugatti stuck to **cable-operated brakes.** This is a far less powerful system, in which the pedal simply pulls on a wire attached to the brake.

When asked why he stuck with cable brakes, Ettore Bugatti showed how single-minded and stubborn he could be. "My cars are made to go," he replied. "They are not made to stop!"

Even with these shortcomings, Bugatti racers and road cars ran, handled, and even stopped with the best of them. They were lightweight and simple. And their solid design gave them the performance they needed.

What's more, the cars were always beautiful to look at. They were often painted in the lush blue that was France's official racing color. One famous Bugatti racer, the Type 35, is thought by some experts to be the most graceful racing machine ever to turn a wheel. It was certainly one of the most successful.

Bugatti had a name for the formula that made his cars what they were. He called them **pur sang.** This term's exact translation is "pure-blooded." But to a French person, the word means "thoroughbred."

Like a champion racehorse or hunting dog (both of which Bugatti raised on his estate), his cars were "bred" without concern about cost or the need to be practical. Instead, each was a work of art, made just as Bugatti ordered it—perfect!

The Type 35 racer proved that Rembrandt Bugatti wasn't the only artist in the family! Modern custom wheels have nothing on these beauties.

6 THE INCREDIBLE ROYALE

Ettore Bugatti was a remarkably proud man. As far as he was concerned, nobody on earth designed or built better cars than he did. If you didn't agree with him, that was your problem. It was this pride that led to the most famous "Bug" of them all...the Type 41 Royale.

There are many tales about how this monumental "car for kings" came to be. The most interesting story tells of a rich Englishwoman and a discussion she had during a dinner with Le Patron. During this chat she supposedly said, "Mr. Bugatti, everyone knows you build the greatest racing and sports cars in the world. But for a town car of *real* elegance, one must go to Rolls-Royce or Daimler, isn't that so?"

No one recorded Bugatti's answer. But we can imagine the hair rising on the back of his neck on hearing such a challenge. We can also imagine him deciding, right then and there, that the best passenger car in the world would come from nowhere but Molsheim. And it would carry the Bugatti name.

In the late 1920s, he set out to build that car. Throwing away his usual ideas on lightness and simple design, he began to scope out his ideas on what would be the most impressive car in the world. He would create a car for kings and queens, a car to rule the road.

As with any car, the design started with the engine. It would be a gigantic straight eight cylinder, some 5 feet long. Imagine an engine longer than a dining room table! Cylinder size ended up at 12.7 liters. This made it one of the largest engines ever built for a car. It was nearly *three times the size of a modern V-8.*

In such an engine, every part was a sight to behold. The pistons were as big as coffee cans. The crankshaft alone weighed 220 **23**

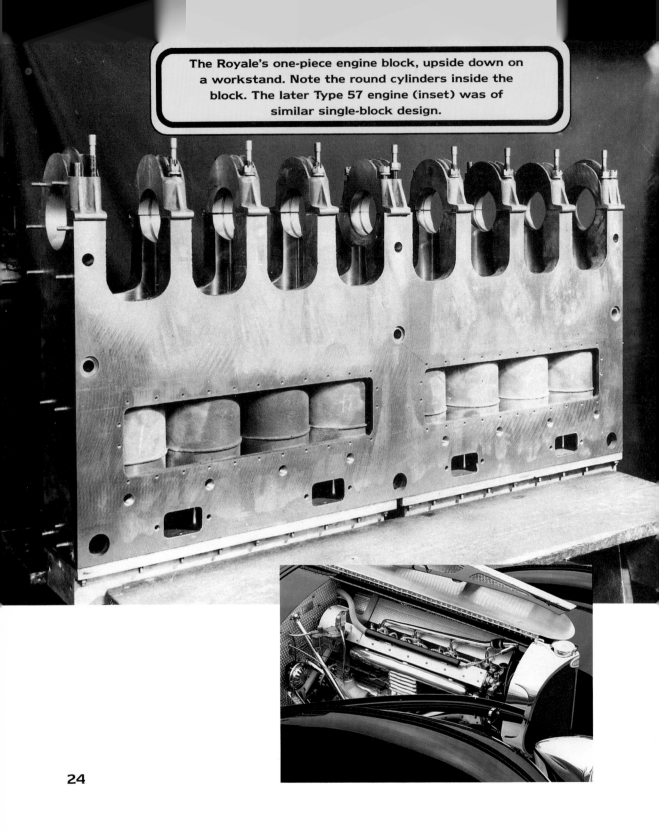

The Royale's one-piece engine block, upside down on a workstand. Note the round cylinders inside the block. The later Type 57 engine (inset) was of similar single-block design.

pounds—as much as a large man. The engine weighed in at a road-shaking 770 pounds. It was heavier than the racecar Bugatti built in 1911!

Seen from the side, a Royale engine is a wall of steel stretching as far as the eye can see. It's also a wall of power. Some say it pumped out between 200 and 300 horsepower at a time when most cars had less than 50 horses under the hood. But the punch came at a slow gallop. It turned at only 1,700 revs per minutes, while most engines turn twice that fast to make their power. That slowness made the Royale a gentle giant that even the most petite princess could drive with ease.

The Royale engine was built with what's called **monobloc** design. If you want to make a mechanic mad, just whisper that word. It means that the engine block is made in one piece, with no separate, easy-to-remove top section. If repairs are needed in this area, the entire engine has to be taken apart from the bottom. Crank and pistons have to be removed. It's a big, dirty job that was made harder by the size and weight of the parts.

Why Bugatti chose this tricky design is a mystery. Perhaps he wanted to make it clear that this car was meant for people with the money to get someone else to do such grungy work for them!

This engine was mounted in a frame that could have served as the skeleton for a skyscraper. It was massive in every way. The steel frame was 10 inches deep in places, and it stretched an incredible length of more than 14 feet, just from front wheel to rear wheel. An entire modern car could park in the space of that frame.

Other parts were sized to go with the engine and frame. The brake drums, for example, are $1^1/2$ feet across. But they were needed to stop the wheels, which were 3 feet tall!

When the **chassis** was completed, the machine was tested. Bugatti drove it to make sure he had indeed built the supercar

The Type 41 "Coupe Napoleon" was the first Royale.
For a while, it was the family car for the Bugattis.

he'd dreamed of. When the test ride was over, he looked at others in the car and smiled. "Good car, eh?" was his only comment. But his remark said it all.

You'll notice that we've said little about the car's body. The reason is that there wasn't one. Bugatti expected his customers to find their own body-building company and to pay extra to get this work done. But there was no discount for buying a half-built car.

Instead, he set the price for the bare chassis and engine far higher than anyone had ever charged for a complete car. It cost an amazing $25,000—a fortune in the 1920s. This was *twice the price* of the most expensive Rolls-Royce of the time, body included—and it was *50 times* what an everyday Ford or Chevy cost. And you still had to get a body built for it!

That's if you could get a Royale chassis at all. Chances are that you couldn't. In his incredible way, Bugatti allowed only the "best people" to place orders...those he personally knew and liked. The king of Spain was "allowed" to ask that one be built, but the king of Albania was not.

Bugatti had met King Zog, it seems, and decided he was not cultured enough to own a Royale. One reason was that Bugatti found the king's table manners "beyond belief."

Of course, you didn't absolutely have to be a king or queen. A Royale was sold to a French baron named Armand Esders, who never drove the car at night. Another was sold to an English doctor.

Bugatti had planned to build 25 to 30 of these land yachts, but his timing was off. The car appeared just as the world was entering the major money crisis called the depression. As factories closed and businesses failed, many of the rich suddenly got a lot poorer. As a result, only six Royales were ever built, two of them becoming Bugatti family cars.

All still exist in museums and collections. When they sell, they sell

Baron Esders's Royale had no headlights! The reason? He never drove at night. The body was designed by Ettore's son Jean.

for prices well up in the millions! Quite simply, the Bugatti Royale has become a legend. It's the king of classics, the most valuable car in the world.

As it happened, no model of the Royale was ever owned by royalty. The king of Spain, who ordered the first Royale, was thrown out of power by his own people before he could take delivery.

But one was owned more recently by a different kind of king, the man who founded Domino's Pizza. He paid more than $8 million to get it. Think of all the pizza Domino's had to sell to pay for that one car!

 7 JEAN BUGATTI

Just as Ettore Bugatti was influenced by his father, so did he influence Jean, his older son. Jean was born in 1909, when Ettore started his company. But this "king's" son was not treated like a prince. Jean was sent to work in the factory almost as soon as he was old enough to hold a wrench. He'd show up at 7 A.M. like every other worker, and he got no special favors. But it was soon clear that he was just as talented as his father at car building, though in a different way.

Where Ettore was a great inventor, Jean was a detail person. He'd make sure the small but important jobs were done well. He was the perfect person to pick up where Ettore's grand dreams left off.

For this reason, Ettore gave Jean a great deal of power at the plant. By the early 1930s, Jean spent as much time designing Bugatti cars as his father did.

There's one model Jean is best known for. It's the famous Type 57.

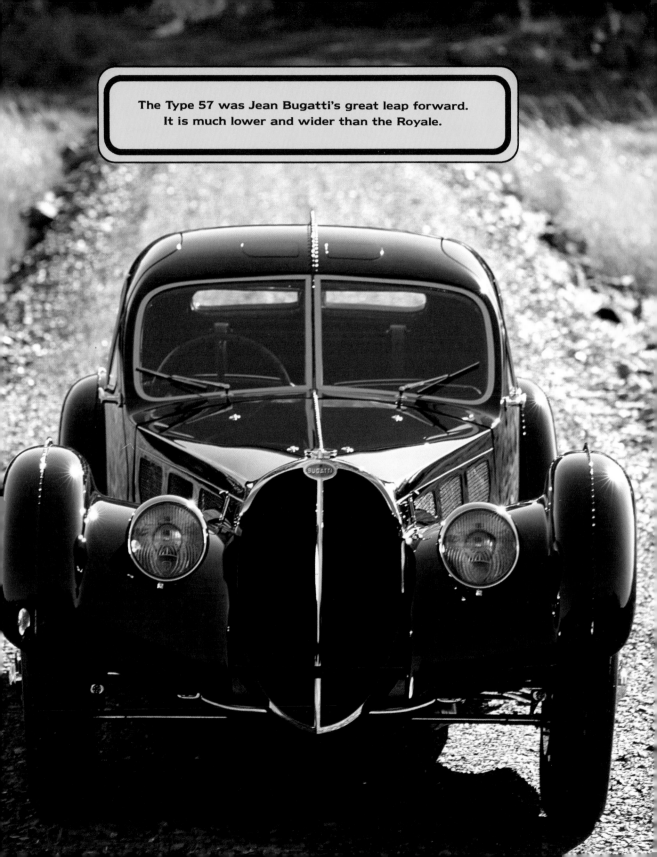

The Type 57 was Jean Bugatti's great leap forward.
It is much lower and wider than the Royale.

First built in 1934, it was the last of a long line of Bugatti's passenger cars produced before World War II shut the plant down. Many experts think it was also Bugatti's best road machine ever.

In its way, the Type 57 showed all that was right about Bugatti and all that was wrong. It was a beautiful machine—it was fast, had great handling, and was built with the finest craftsmanship. The engine was a modern 3.3-liter eight cylinder, with **twin overhead camshafts.** This is a system that opens and closes the valves faster for more power. Some models also had a **super-charger,** a pump that rams gas and air right down the engine's throat, giving even more horses from the same-size engine.

But Bugatti put such inventions on his engines later than other automakers, and there were other improvements he still refused to make. As with almost every Bugatti ever built, the Type 57 still had the old solid front axle. And most 57s also had cable-operated brakes.

It was clear this wasn't the way Jean wanted it. He'd built the first Type 57 with independent suspension, but his father ordered it off the car. "Such a thing is not proper for a Bugatti!" Ettore told his 23-year-old son.

In one way, however, the Type 57 was a major improvement over past Bugattis. The car offered a full line of fabulous body styles, in two doors or four. Buyers could order anything from a racy two-seat sportster to a luxury sedan. They could also order one of the most daring designs ever produced by any automaker—the Type 57 Atlantic Coupe.

There's never been another car like the Atlantic. At that time, it was the most streamlined road car ever built. It looked like some giant smooth-skinned beetle about to pounce. And it was built of a special lightweight metal instead of the usual steel.

Because this metal was hard to bend into the tight curves of small parts, the body was made in two large halves. Then those two halves were riveted together down the middle. There was a ridge where the halves met, much like a walnut shell. It started at the radiator, continued to the windshield, and went right over the top and down to the back bumper. This unusual "fin" has never been seen on any other car, and it makes a Type 57 Atlantic easy to identify.

At least it would be easy to identify if there were more of them. As it happens, only three Atlantics were ever built. All are priceless, and seldom do they leave the museums or well-warmed garages where they are kept.

The Atlantic Coupe was the first car with a tailfin. These fins were born for engineering reasons, not just style.

8   TROUBLED TIMES

Through the 1920s and into the 1930s, everything went right for Ettore Bugatti. He seemed to lead a charmed life, with never-ending success in both business and racing. Each day he'd ride the grounds of his great estate like a monarch, visiting his racehorses and hunting dogs, giving orders and taking the salutes of his employees.

In fact, he lived a king's life. He visited with royalty and always enjoyed the finest in foods and wines, some of which were made from grapes in his own vineyards. He also collected artwork, including the animal sculptures made by his brother, Rembrandt, for which he built a private museum right on the grounds.

Bugatti was known to present his children with special gifts. When his younger son, Roland, wanted a ride-around model car, he got a tiny version of a Bugatti racing machine. Called the Type 52, it was powered by a battery instead of a gasoline engine. Otherwise, it was perfectly engineered and built just like the real thing. The toy was so popular that Ettore had the factory build more of them. They were given to the children of some of his rich friends. There was even a track in Argentina where the Type 52 was raced!

Then, in the mid-1930s, Bugatti's luck changed. From that point onward, everything seemed to go wrong. The troubles began when the Royale, into which Ettore had sunk so much time and money, did not sell well. Always inventive, Bugatti soon found another use for the monster engine he'd created for the car. He went to France's railroads with the suggestion of powering trains with it.

His idea was to build a superlight, self-powered passenger car for short-distance service. "Use my machine," he told railway

Even the toy Bugattis got a number—Type 52.

managers, "instead of a clumsy, expensive-to-run steam engine for this kind of job. You'll gain speed and save money!"

The railroads loved it. And by the mid-1930s Bugatti was in the railroad-car-engine business. It seemed as if his troubles would be short-lived after all.

As he'd hoped, the new rail car was a huge success. With twin Royale eights for power, a Bugatti rail car could carry 107 passengers at close to 100 miles per hour. With its light weight, it gained speed faster and stopped easier than any rail car ever. And in a test run, with Jean at the controls, it hit 124 miles per hour, breaking every steam engine record in the book.

Passengers loved the streamlined look Bugatti gave the rail car. And they were thrilled with the sleek, silent train trips. They no longer had to suffer from the black smoke and flying ashes that went with steam-engined trains.

The good times were not going to last, however. To build the big rail cars, Ettore had to expand his factory to more than 1,000 workers. There was no time slowly and carefully to teach the new employees the Bugatti way and create the loyalty his workers had always had for Le Patron. Instead, the new workers put in long hours for what they felt was not enough pay.

One day in 1936, it all bubbled over. Bugatti workers went on strike, shutting down the factory. Even worse, when Ettore tried to enter, his own employees barred the way.

Ettore Bugatti was an artist, not a businessman. He had no idea how to handle the strike. Instead, he took it personally. Deeply hurt, he simply told the workers that if they no longer wanted his leadership, he would leave Molsheim and never return.

Bugatti was serious about this threat. Within days, he'd packed his belongings, and he and his family moved to Paris, leaving Jean in charge.

Under Ettore's more practical son, work soon resumed, but worse times were to come. On the evening of August 11, 1939, Jean was testing a new car on a road near the plant. He'd done test drives before. This night, however, someone else was on the road. It was a postman on a bicycle, later found to be quite drunk. The man had been warned that a racing car was performing high-speed tests somewhere out there, yet he was pedaling right up the center line, in total darkness.

As it happened, Jean rounded a bend, suddenly saw the man, and swerved to avoid him. The Bugatti skidded out of control and tumbled into a ditch. Jean was killed instantly.

When Ettore learned that his beloved son was dead at age 30, his grief was unstoppable. But his troubles were far from over. Just three weeks later, World War II broke out. Molsheim was again in the path of the march. But this time, the marchers were Nazi storm troopers.

 ## 9 FIGHTING THE NAZIS

When the Germans threatened to invade France, Bugatti immediately met with French government leaders to discuss what to do. They decided to move the factory machines and workers to Bordeaux, a city far from the border. There they would make aircraft engines for French warplanes.

This move was carried out. But within a year, Germany had taken over all of France. The Bugatti works were now under Nazi control, and his factory was ordered to make war machines for the German armies.

Ettore was now 60 years old and living in Paris. He began a weird double life. To outsiders—and Nazi secret police—he was an old, sick, retired man living quietly in his apartment.

But one floor below, he'd secretly brought together a team of his best designers and engineers. Behind closed curtains, they worked on new designs for the day when the Germans would be driven out and the factory could again produce machines of speed and beauty.

Cars were on the drawing boards, but so were futuristic aircraft and boats. Even Hitler could not stop the flood of Bugatti's ideas. Not all those ideas were peaceful. Several of Bugatti's workers were involved in the **Resistance,** a secret group that took action

This beautiful coupe shows why Bugattis are so admired. Compare it with the lumpy designs of other carmarkers in the 1930s.

against the Germans. Le Patron fully supported them, offering shelter and money.

One of those men was a race driver named Robert Benoist. His story deserves telling, partly because one of the heroes of the tale is a Bugatti car!

Benoist was at the wheel of a Type 57 roadster on a trip to join up with other Resistance fighters when he ran smack into a German tank division. The Germans captured him, and one of the officers fell in love with the car.

Benoist, who looked and acted like a civilian, was ordered to fall in line with the tanks and drive the prize to German headquarters. There the officer would get the car. Benoist thought he would probably get shot!

For a day and a night, Benoist traveled with his captors. German guns were pointed at him. He even got a fuel refill along with the tanks. Then the group reached a crossing where a deserted country road led off to the left of the main highway.

Benoist knew that if he could get to that road before the Germans let loose a hail of bullets, he might be able to escape. He waited and waited for just the right moment. Then, as the Germans slowed down to avoid some traffic, he saw his chance. He slammed the car into low gear, turned sharply left, and floored the twin-cam engine. Before the Germans could react, the Bugatti was slipping and sliding away. Kicking up sand and dust, the car sped off at over 100 miles an hour!

Benoist didn't let up until he'd reached a friend's farm, where he hid the car. He was able to join his unit and continue the fight— thanks to the help of one very fast Bugatti.

Sadly, Benoist was hanged as a French spy a few years later. But he was a hero to the end. On the cell wall, jailers found a message he had written to other prisoners. "Never confess! R.B."

10) ETTORE'S LAST BATTLE

When the war ended in 1945, Ettore Bugatti was ready to go back to work. He planned to return to his factory and put some of his dreams into motion. But one final nightmare now faced him.

Because the Germans had used his factory, it was called "enemy property." The factory was handed over to the French government. And because Bugatti had been born an Italian and Italy had joined Germany in the war, he was told he couldn't have it back. "If you don't like what we're doing, go to court!" government officials told him.

So Bugatti began a costly and brutal two-year battle. There were many lawyers and papers and legal bills to deal with. And when one court ruled against him, he had to go through the same thing with another court. Finally a decision came down in his favor. The government was ordered to return the factory to Bugatti ownership.

That night, he drove home alone. He climbed the stairs to his room...and never came down again. A few weeks later, on August 21, 1947, Le Patron died at age 65. He was a sad but never really broken man. He'd lived life his way, and the automobile world was better for it.

As the court had ordered, the factory was returned to the family. For several years, it produced rail cars and other machinery. And for a short time in 1951, Bugatti's younger son, Roland, produced a car called the Type 101. Money was tight, though, and only six of the cars were built.

Finally, in the 1960s, what was left of the company was bought by a French aircraft engine maker. The name Bugatti was taken off the wall. The workshops are still in Molsheim. But you won't find the name of the founder anywhere on them.

11 THE CAR THAT REFUSED TO DIE!

When the Bugatti works were purchased, it seemed as though the sale marked the end of the famous car. In time, Bugatti would be forgotten, as so many other car builders had been. But then a surprising thing happened. The car's followers would not let the Bugatti name die.

In the 1920s the first Bugatti owners' clubs were formed. Even after the cars were no longer being built, the fan clubs grew stronger. Each year more books were written about Bugatti. Fans kept track of every single car—where it was, who owned it, and how well it was being taken care of. And a few designers drew pictures or made models of what a brand-new Bugatti might be like, even though few seriously thought there would ever be such a car.

They were wrong.

Jump forward in time to the summer of 1990. The place is Paris. The event is a gathering of classic Bugatti cars and their owners for a special moment. They've come to see the introduction of a brand-new Bugatti.

How did it happen? Somehow, wealthy supporters gathered millions of dollars to start their own car company. They bought the rights to use the name and the famous red oval "EB" symbol. They built a modern factory in Italy. And they hired top engineering talent. Now the result of their efforts was on display.

Sitting on a Paris street that day was a sleek blue bullet of a machine as wild looking as any Ferrari or Lamborghini. Barely waist high, it had wide tires and slick **alloy** wheels. And it was covered with powerful-looking vents and slots. In short, it looked like a true supercar, but one with the familiar horseshoe-shaped radiator opening on the front.

Under its lightweight skin beat the heart of a supercar. The new "Bugatti EB 110" (the car would be presented to the public in 1991, on the *110th* anniversary of Bugatti's birth) was powered by a totally new, 60-valve 3.5-liter V-12 engine. It had *four* **turbochargers** and was said to produce over 500 horsepower. This power was fed to the road through four-wheel drive...something seen on no other supercar except Porsche's rare and costly 959 "supercar of the future."

Top speed was promised at more than 210 miles per hour. At this pace, the new Bugatti would be one of the fastest road cars in the world.

What's more, this wasn't even the hot version. A Super Sport model was later shown, with 50 more horsepower and an even higher top speed. The speedometer read all the way to 248 miles per hour!

And the price?

As they say in the supercar business, if you have to ask, you can't afford one. But we'll tell you anyway. The car was expected to land in the garage of its lucky owners at more than half a million dollars a copy.

It was 1992 before the magazine writers could get an EB 110 to test. But when they did, the car delivered as promised. "The power is something we can't easily explain," wrote one dazed reporter after a ride. "A big hand pushes your entire body into the seat, your head into the headrest. You can't compare it to any other sports car. The closest thing is when an airplane enters an air pocket. If you have the courage and craziness to stay on the gas," the reporter wrote, "this is one car you can fly."

At this time, no one knows the fate of the new machine. Will the

Bugatti lives! Though Ettore had no part in the EB110, his spirit is all over this supercar.

MIAMI DOLPHINS

BY BARRY WILNER

The Child's World®

Published by The Child's World®
1980 Lookout Drive • Mankato, MN 56003-1705
800-599-READ • www.childsworld.com

Acknowledgments
The Child's World®: Mary Berendes, Publishing Director
Red Line Editorial: Editorial direction
The Design Lab: Design
Amnet: Production

Design Element: Dean Bertoncelj/Shutterstock Images
Photographs ©: Lynne Sladky/AP Images, cover; Kevin
Terrell/AP Images, 5, 27; Bill Wippert/AP Images, 7; AP
Images, 9; Bill Kostroun/AP Images, 11; Richard Cavalleri/
Shutterstock Images, 13; Doug Murray/AP Images, 14-15;
Horace Court/AP Images, 17; Jeff Glidden/AP Images, 19;
Wilfredo Lee/AP Images, 21; Ben Liebenberg/NFL
Photos/AP Images, 23; Rick Osentoski/AP Images, 25;
Tom DiPace/AP Images, 29

ISBN 9781631439889
LCCN 2014959658

Printed in the United States of America
Mankato, MN
July, 2015
PAO2265

ABOUT THE AUTHOR

Barry Wilner has written more than 40 books, including many for young readers. He is a sports writer for the Associated Press and has covered such events as the Super Bowl, Olympics, and World Cup. He lives in Garnerville, New York.

TABLE OF CONTENTS

GO, DOLPHINS!

The Miami Dolphins started as an **expansion** team. Expansion teams are not usually very good at first. But the Dolphins got off to a fast start. Running back Joe Auer returned the first kickoff in Dolphins' history for a **touchdown**. And within only seven years, the Dolphins became the best team in the league. They have since had many more great moments. Let's meet the Miami Dolphins.

Dolphins defensive end Cameron Wake rushes into the backfield in a game against the Denver Broncos on November 23, 2014.